DESIGN AND MAINTENANCE
OF ACCOUNTING MANUALS

**THE WILEY INSTITUTE OF MANAGEMENT ACCOUNTANTS
PROFESSIONAL BOOK SERIES**

Jack Fox • *Starting and Building Your Own Accounting Business, Second Edition*

Harry L. Brown • *Design and Maintenance of Accounting Manuals, Second Edition*

Gordon V. Smith • *Business Valuation: A Manager's Guide*

James A. Brimson • *Activity Accounting: An Activity-Based Costing Approach*

DESIGN AND MAINTENANCE OF ACCOUNTING MANUALS

Second Edition

1994 Supplement

Harry L. Brown, CPA, CDP

JOHN WILEY & SONS, INC.

New York • Chichester • Brisbane • Toronto • Singapore

This text is printed on acid-free paper.

Copyright © 1994 by John Wiley & Sons, Inc.

All rights reserved. Published simultaneously in Canada.

Reproduction or translation of any part of this work beyond that permitted by Section 107 or 108 of the 1976 United States Copyright Act without the permission of the copyright owner is unlawful. Requests for permission or further information should be addressed to the Permissions Department, John Wiley & Sons, Inc., 605 Third Avenue, New York, NY 10158-0012.

This publication is designed to provide accurate and authoritative information in regard to the subject matter covered. It is sold with the understanding that the publisher is not engaged in rendering legal, accounting, or other professional services. If legal advice or other expert assistance is required, the services of a competent professional person should be sought.

Library of Congress Cataloging in Publication Data:

Brown, Harry L.
    Design and maintenance of accounting manuals / Harry L. Brown.—
2nd ed.
       p.   cm.—(The Wiley/Institute of Management Accountants professional book series)
    Includes index.
    ISBN 0-471-59643-4 (cloth)
    ISBN 0-471-01029-4 (supplement)
    1. Accounting—Handbooks, manuals, etc.—Authorship. I. Title.
  II. Series.
    HF5657.B75   1993
    808'.066657—dc20   92-45032

Printed in the United States of America

10 9 8 7 6 5 4 3 2 1

ACKNOWLEDGMENTS

Much of the material in Chapter 3A has been reprinted with permission from *Internal Control—Integrated Framework,* Copyright © 1992 by the Committee of Sponsoring Organizations of the Treadway Commission:

- Text material where noted.
- Figures 3A.2, 3A.5, 3A.6, 3A.7, 3A.8, 3A.9, 3A.10, 3A.11, 3A.12, 3A.13

The common grammar and usage problems material in Chapter 10, with minor changes, has been reprinted with permission from *A Guide for Wiley Interscience and Ronald Press Authors in the Preparation and Production of Manuscript and Illustrations,* Copyright © 1974, 1979 by John Wiley & Sons, Inc.

PREFACE

The new chapter in this first supplement to *Design and Maintenance of Accounting Manuals,* Second Edition, shows how to initiate an internal control procedure system based on the Committee of Sponsoring Organizations of the Treadway Commission's four-volume series, *Internal Control—Integrated Framework.* The Committee recommends that management report to its stockholders in its management reports, and that organizations have the independent auditors attest to the internal control as it exists at the time. There will be objections to the study and some controversy is expected; however, it appears that action to implement the reporting of internal control, and attestation thereof by independent accountants, will become a reality in the near future.

Also covered in this 1994 supplement are sections on other uses of the policy/procedure system, documenting personal computer operations, and some additional common grammar and usage problems, particularly rules of abbreviation (including the latest postal abbreviations), capitalization, and other punctuation rules.

With the nationwide reduction in middle management personnel to produce competitive cost savings, documenting current operations becomes even more important. "I came; I saw; I documented." is something to remember and to live by. Write on!

HARRY L. BROWN

Traverse City, Michigan
December 1993

SUPPLEMENT CONTENTS

Note to the Reader: Materials that appear only in the supplement and not in the bound volume are indicated by "(New)" after the title.

CHAPTER 3
POLICY/PROCEDURE
STATEMENTS:
YOU DO SOMETHING
TO ME

Page 55, add at end of chapter:

OTHER USES OF THE P/PS SYSTEM (NEW)

The policy/procedure statement system is ideally suited for other manuals which are related in some ways to accounting operations. These manuals are the *purchasing manual, human resources manual (personnel),* and the *data processing manual.* They are developed, distributed, and maintained by the directors or managers of the respective departments. These systems should provide labeled binders to user departments and consider using a special paper color to differentiate from other P/PS systems in use by the company. Other related systems that could be used by purchasing, human resources, and data processing are the *forms manual* (Chapter 4), *user manual (employee handbook)* (Chapter 7), and the *information release system* (Chapter 8).

Purchasing.   Because of the variety of goods and services needed by an entity, and the involvement of the purchasing department in all these acquisitions, purchasing manuals are difficult to write and even more difficult to maintain. There is no question that current purchasing documentation is needed by all other departments in the company.

Most purchasing departments rewrite the department manual every year or two, a burdensome task and one sometimes delayed for years for that reason. When this happens, employees begin to rely on verbal instructions, previously prepared documents, and information received from employees other than purchasing personnel.

The policy/procedure statement system is an ideal tool to develop and maintain a comprehensive purchasing handbook. The P/PS Manual is not an employee handbook, but rather a department handbook, with one copy placed in each using department for reference by the employees in that department. The *purchasing manual* could be developed as follows, with retrieval number groups assigned to major sections.

Initiation and general information

Purchase requisitions

Supplies

Services

Nonreceiving services (repairs, publications, etc.)

Vendor approval

Standing orders

Purchase order drafts

Receiving:

   Full delivery

   Partial delivery

   Checking counts and weights

Developing specifications

Bidding procedures:

   Small bidding orders

   Large bidding orders

Error follow-up and disposition

Controlling make-or-buy decisions

The format of purchasing policy/procedure statements is identical to the accounting system previously described.

Human Resources.   The *human resources policy/procedure statement* system is similar to the old employee handbook, with one exception—it is not issued to all employees, but is distributed to each department for reference purposes and use by the employees in each department. An outline of its contents could be as follows:

Initiation and general information

Interview techniques and prohibited questions

Hiring

Probation

Transfer

Termination

Unions

Classifications and pay levels

Longevity pay and bonuses

Fringe benefits:

    Social Security

    Pension plan

    Eyeglass insurance

    Child care

    Cafeteria plan

    Dental insurance

Vacation, holiday, and special leave

Sickness

Jury duty, military leave

Forms—application, payroll, and other

Most distributions of these P/PSs would be to departments, although there may be an occasional distribution to "All Employees" or "Designated." Development and maintenance would be similar to accounting policies and procedures.

Data Processing.   The *data processing policy/procedure statement* system differs from that shown in Chapter 6, although most of that information could be incorporated into this suggested manual. This manual would be primarily concerned with the day-to-day operations of the data processing or computer department. Following is a suggested outline of this manual.

Facilities:

    Access control

    Security provisions (fire and other)

    Backup hardware procedures

Personnel:

    Job titles, salary ranges, and minimum education and background

    Hiring, promotion, and transfer

Input processing control

Computer processing control

File control and off-premises backup

Output processing control

Terminal use and control

Personal computers:
    Hardware security
    Data security (passwords)
    Program approvals and security
    Data backup procedures
Documentation requirements:
    Purchased programs
    In-house programs
Program changes
Service requests:
    Processing failures
    Program additions, deletions, changes
    New program requests
User documentation standards

The *data processing policy/procedure statement* manual would be developed and maintained the same as the accounting manuals. However, much of its contents would be held only in data processing. Those policies and procedures needed by user departments would be issued at the department level and available to those employees in each department with a need to know or use.

CHAPTER 3A
INTERNAL CONTROL:
HAPPY TRAILS TO YOU
(NEW)

This chapter shows how the policy/procedure statement (P/PS) system can be used to implement comprehensive internal control reviews of an organization. The entire chapter is based on *Internal Control—Integrated Framework,* published by the Committee of Sponsoring Organizations (COSO) of the Treadway Commission in September 1992. The four-volume *Internal Control—Integrated Framework* (Product code #990002) may be obtained from the Order Department, American Institute of Certified Public Accountants, Harborside Financial Center, 201 Plaza III, Jersey City, NJ 07311-3881. Toll-free telephone 1-800-862-4272; fax 1-800-362-5066.

Internal Control—Integrated Framework was prepared in response to recommendations of the National Commission on Fraudulent Financial Reporting, commonly referred to as the Treadway Commission. It was sponsored by the American Accounting Association, the American Institute of Certified Public Accountants, the Financial Executives Institute, the Institute of Internal Auditors, and the Institute of Management Accountants. The Commission's report, issued in 1987, recommended that the sponsoring organizations develop additional, integrated guidance on internal control to provide a common reference point which entities can use to assess the quality of their internal control systems. *Internal Control—Integrated Framework* is the result of that recommendation.

EXECUTIVE SUMMARY

The Executive Summary describes the four volumes of *Internal Control—Integrated Framework* as follows:

The first is this *Executive Summary* (7 pages), a high-level overview of the internal control framework directed to the chief executive and other senior executives, board members, legislators and regulators.

The second volume, the *Framework* (118 pages), defines internal control, describes its components and provides criteria against which managements, boards, or other can assess their control systems. The *Executive Summary* is included.

The third volume, *Reporting to External Parties* (25 pages), is a supplemental document providing guidance to those entities that report publicly on internal control over preparation of their published financial statements, or are contemplating doing so.

The fourth volume, *Evaluation Tools* (203 pages), provides materials that may be useful in conducting an evaluation of an internal control system.

DEFINING INTERNAL CONTROL

The Executive Summary defines *internal control* as follows:

Internal control means different things to different people. This causes confusion among businesspeople, legislators, regulators and others. Resulting miscommunication and different expectations cause problems within an enterprise. Problems are compounded when the term, if not clearly defined, is written into law, regulation or rule.

This report deals with the needs and expectations of management and others. It defines and describes internal control to:

- Establish a common definition serving the needs of different parties.
- Provide a standard against which business and other entities—large or small, in the public or private sector, for profit or not—can assess their control systems and determine how to improve them.

Internal control is broadly defined as a process, effected by an entity's board of directors, management and other personnel, designed to provide reasonable assurance regarding the achievement of objectives in the following categories.

- Effectiveness and efficiency of operations.
- Reliability of financial reporting.
- Compliance with applicable laws and regulations.

The first category addresses an entity's basic business objectives, including performance and profitability goals and safeguarding of resources. The second relates to the preparation of reliable published financial statements, including interim and condensed financial statements and selected financial data derived from such statements, such as earnings releases, reported publicly. The third deals with complying with those laws and regulations to which the entity is subject. These distinct but overlapping categories address different needs and allow a directed focus to meet the separate needs.

The report emphasizes these three categories in many places in the report. The author disagrees, and sees little difference between operational controls and financial controls— about the same as the difference between a "doughnut" and a "fried-cake." Historically, internal control has always been within the province of the accounting and financial personnel; in fact, it is usually included in the job descriptions of these employees.

Accountants are trained to be alert to weaknesses and breaks in internal control and, more importantly, they are interested in control procedures and functions. Therefore, this chapter considers operational and financial controls as one group of controls.

THE INTERNAL CONTROL REVIEW

Up to now, most internal control reviews have been related to financial statement items, assets, liabilities, equity, income, and expense. See Figure 3A.1. They then turn to the departmental functions involved in handling these accounts. COSO changes the emphasis by relating internal control reviews to control components and functional departments such as accounting, human resources, computer services, and so on. This change in emphasis will not change how reviews are done or reported to upper management and others. Reviews will continue to be done by employees within a department, by accounting personnel, the internal auditors, and external certified public accountants as part of the annual audit.

Initiating the Internal Control System

If you decide not to use an existing policy/procedure system, or if no such system is in place, then the internal control policy/procedure system should be initiated. It follows all of the starting procedures discussed in Chapter 3. For illustrative purposes in this book, the system name is "Internal Control Policy/Procedure." Any other suitable name can be chosen, such as "Internal Control," "Internal Control Administration," "Internal Control Reviews," and so on.

The first release, announcing the program, should describe the layout and contents of all such future releases. See Figure 3A.4 (Retrieval No. 001). The board of directors, senior officers, and department heads should be issued a looseleaf binder to hold the ICP/P statements. The "Information Release" system (Chapter 8) can be used to announce the new internal control policy/procedure system. Distribution of this release can be to *all employees* or *department heads and above.*

For the internal control policy/procedure figures in this chapter, the following 3-digit Retrieval Numbers will be used:

001-099	General statements
100-199	Executive Summary Policy/Procedure statements
200-399	Framework Policy/Procedure statements
400-499	Reporting to External Parties Policy/Procedure statements
500-699	Evaluation Tools Policy/Procedure statements
700-999	Available

The development of additional internal control procedures is an evolutionary process which will be developed and added to slowly. Hence, this numbering scheme should be

General Account Category	Related Internal Control Procedures
Cash	Receipts control Disbursements control Reconcilement
Investments	Depository control Buy and sell control
Accounts Receivable	Authorization control Receipts control Billing control Reconcilement
Notes Receivable	Same as accounts receivable
Inventory	Purchasing control Receiving control Usage control Cost procedures Shipping control
Land, Buildings, Equipment, Leasehold Improvements	Legal contracts control (deeds and rental agreements) Acquisition, transfer, and disposal control Maintenance control
Accounts Payable, Accrued Expenses	Purchasing authorization control Receiving control Vendor control Travel expense control
Bonds Payable	Unissued bonds control Issued bonds control Interest payment control
Stockholders' Equity	Unissued certificates control Stockholder registration control
Sales	Customer authorization Cash and credit control Returns and allowances control
Cost of Goods Sold	Payroll control Inventory control Cost Procedures and variances Purchasing control
Expenses	Purchase acqisition and approval Legal contracts Reasonableness control Department budget control Returns and allowances control Bondholder registers (interest)

Figure 3A.1.   Internal control reviews by account category.

adequate for many years. However, other numbering schemes may be used, either a 4-digit or a 5-digit separate series, or a series incorporated into the regular policy/procedure statement system by assigning a group of numbers to this project.

The initial release is self-explanatory except for the *index* (see Figure 3A.3, Retrieval No. INDEX) and *attachments.* The index is released periodically, usually after a half-dozen or so new retrieval numbers have been issued. When a retrieval number has been superseded or deleted since the last index was issued, it will be listed and the replacement retrieval number or the word "Deleted" shown. On all subsequent index releases, the superseded number will not be shown, indicating it is no longer in effect and should be removed from the binder.

Attachments are not given a retrieval page number. They are attached and referred to at the end of the last page of the release. Attachments can be other company documents, forms, laws or other outside documents, and anything else that explains or is related to the material being provided.

Roles and Responsibilities

The roles of various participants in the internal control process are enumerated in Figure 3A.5 (Retrieval No. 100). This release also defines what internal control can and cannot do; these definitions should be kept in mind during the entire internal control review and evaluation process. It also explains that all employees in the entity have some responsibility for internal control.

Also defined herein are the five interrelated components of internal control: Control Environment; Risk Assessment; the diverse Control Activities that are in use or in place; Information and Communication; and Monitoring, which means that any deficiencies must be reported to a higher level, possibly as high as top management or the board of directors.

Glossary

A glossary of 34 terms, all related to the contents of *Internal Control—Integrated Framework,* can be helpful. See Figure 3A.6 (Retrieval No. 200). Additional terms should be added to the glossary as questions on meanings and definitions arise during the review process. The definitions in the glossary are tightly written, and it may be necessary to expand on the definitions therein or show examples of meanings. In the author's opinion, the definition of "operations" should be added to "financial reporting."

Annual Report on Internal Control

This release (Figure 3A.7, Retrieval No. 400) explains the format of a report to the stockholders and others as part of the annual or other published financial reports. Any company of significant size should have an audit committee within the board of directors. If this or a similar committee is in place and is active, that fact should be mentioned in the report. If this internal control system and/or a regular policy/procedure statement system is active, then the mention thereof should be part of the management report.

Other items to be included are organizational reporting relationships and division of responsibility, and personnel recruiting, selection, training, and development. If in place, the entity's code of conduct should be explained, along with compliance reporting methods and the existence and effectiveness of an internal audit department. The *Journal of Accountancy,* August 1993, contains the Statement on Standards for Attestation Engagements Number 2, *Reporting on an Entity's Internal Control Structure Over Financial Reporting.* Although this Statement deals only with the independent auditor's attestation regarding the entity's internal controls, much of the information contained therein is closely related to the information provided by *Internal Control—Integrated Framework.* The Statement was effective "for an examination of management's assertion on the effectiveness of an entity's internal control structure over financial reporting when the assertion is as of December 15, 1993 or thereafter."

EVALUATION TOOLS

Control Environment

Although written in a slightly different format, the headings and subheadings in this release are basically a program of examination of internal control (PEIC). See Figure 3A.8 (Retrieval No. 500). This statement is true of all the Retrieval 500 series which follow. A PEIC should be prepared prior to any review and evaluation of an internal control procedure. Before any program of examination is used, it should be reviewed for its appropriateness and completeness by the chief executive officer or someone assigned by the CEO to do so. Senior management approval should be a requisite for all programs of examination.

Each program point of focus should be answered by the evaluator during the course of the engagement. The evaluator also determines and indicates the risk associated with each major item in the review and evaluation.

Risk Assessment

This release (Figure 3A.9, Retrieval No. 501) is also the basis of a program of examination, in this case to review and evaluate the entity's risks, and determine that adequate objectives are being set for all activities and major processes within the entity. This program should provide for identifying risks from external sources and the adequacy of management's mechanisms to identify these risks. After identification of risks, there should be a means of estimating the severity of the risk, determining whether each risk is likely to occur, and what can be done to minimize or eliminate the risk.

Control Activities

Figure 3A.10 (Retrieval No. 502) relates directly to the purpose of initiating this internal control policy/procedure system. Appropriate policies and procedures must be developed over time for each of the various activities of the company. After development, management must follow up to make sure that described controls are being used and are effective.

Information and Communication

This release defines a manual information system that provides internal and external information and informs specific employees with the information so they can handle responsibilities in an efficient and effective manner. See Figure 3A.11 (Retrieval 503). It suggests the use of an information technology steering committee of executives. This committee would be responsible not only for gathering information, but also for communicating the information through meetings, supervision, and formal and informal training sessions. A two-way channel should be established to ease communications among the employees, outsiders, and senior executives so problems can be resolved as soon as they arise.

Monitoring

Monitoring the internal control system consists of all the ongoing activities of employees that assure the controls are still in place and in use. See Figure 3A.12 (Retrieval No. 504). Much of the monitoring consists of periodic checks of the assets on hand with the recorded amounts of those assets (for example, securities, inventory, physical properties, and so on). Significant monitoring can be accomplished by an effective internal audit department that has access to the board of directors. The internal audit function should develop audit plans and programs which are suitable to the organization's needs. A communication system that provides for adequate monitoring should include written policies and procedures, current organization charts, and operating instructions for employees.

RISK ASSESSMENT AND CONTROL ACTIVITIES WORKSHEET

The Risk Assessment and Control Activities Worksheet has been illustrated in the Evaluation Tools volume. See Figure 3A.13 (Retrieval 505). Although the worksheet provides an excellent document with which to summarize an evaluation of an activity, its size would make it difficult to use in completing an evaluation, particularly in interviews with affected employees. To provide adequate space for handwritten comments, the form would have to be double-wide, at least 15 to 17 inches.

The author has designed a replacement form, 8½ by 11 inches. See Figure 3A.2. The preprinted form (boldface characters) would be used to enter the program of examination steps to be followed, each numbered consecutively for that specific evaluation. The rest of the form would be completed manually during the observations, interviews, and discussions necessary in evaluating a procedure or process. With one audit step per page, much paper would be generated, but, as the author learned on his first independent audit, "supplies are cheap, time is expensive."

The form would be completed as follows:

Activity. Enter the formal name of the task being evaluated.

Objective. Enter, prior to the visit, the objective (program of examination step) to be covered during the evaluation.

Operations, Financial Reporting, Compliance. The evaluator, after completing the evaluation, circles which of the objective category or categories are appropriate.

Risk Analysis—Factors. The evaluator enters one or more factors that may affect the objective being studied.

Actions, Control Activities, Comments. All findings are written here by the evaluator.

Evaluation and Conclusion. The evaluator's final evaluation and conclusions are written here, including the evaluator's opinion as to whether the procedures are adequate or inadequate to reach the objective listed.

If this substitute document is preferred, it would become the attachment in Figure 3A.13, in place of the larger worksheet from the "Evaluation Tools" volume.

OVERALL INTERNAL CONTROL SYSTEM EVALUATION

Finally, a form is used to complete the evaluator's overall evaluation. See Figure 3A.14 (Retrieval 506). This two-column form contains the total objective of the study just completed, and space for additional considerations, risk assessment, control activities, information and communication, monitoring, and, most importantly, the overall conclusion of the evaluator(s).

SUMMARY

If an organization plans to implement a thorough study of its internal control, it is looking forward to considerable effort by its board, its senior officers, its internal audit

RISK ASSESSMENT AND CONTROL ACTIVITIES WORKSHEET

Activity: INBOUND MATERIALS - MANAGEMENT LOGISTICS

Objectives:

1. Materials are to be tested, and either accepted or moved to storage, or rejected and returned for credit on a timely basis.

(Operations,) **Financial Reporting, Compliance (Circle applicable area).**

Risk Analysis - Factors:

Receipt of large quantities of materials may delay the receiving and testing activities.

Risk Analysis - Likelihood: *Medium-High*

Actions, Control Activities, Comments:

A. *Production provides a weekly report of those items most critically needed to continue efficient and uninterrupted production. The Director of Procurement reviews materials to be tested and prioritizes such materials based on the weekly report.*

B. *Certain engineering personnel have been trained and are available for short-term use in testing certain types of materials.*

Evaluation and Conclusion

Policies and procedures are insufficient for timely processing. Policies and procedures must be developed to detail how materials should flow through receiving and testing, in the event of large amounts of material being received, and how the achievement of the objective is to be monitored. Additionally, using engineering personnel to test materials may create conflicts between testing and engineering, especially if such use negatively affects achievement of engineering objectives.

Figure 3A.2. Replacement "Risk Assessment and Control Activities Worksheet" form.

staff, and all employees. Instituting a well-planned policy/procedure system as outlined in this chapter should provide a sound base for beginning the project, for informing employees of the future plans of the organization, and in communicating with all parties that will become involved.

NOTE AT THE END

You should not be left with the impression that *Internal Control—Integrated Framework* is a finished product, ready to be accepted by all as the final answer to the study of internal control in business organizations. In a letter to COSO, Donald H. Chapin, Assistant Comptroller General, General Accounting Office, objected to any adoption of the COSO report *Internal Control—Integrated Framework* without additional legislation. Chapin says the COSO report

1. Does not advocate public reporting on internal controls for financial reporting and fails to encourage evaluation of other controls, such as those for laws and regulations.
2. Excludes safeguarding of assets from financial reporting controls, which is actually a step backward from those controls long associated with financial reporting.
3. Does not recognize the important roles that an entity's external auditor can play in evaluating internal controls.
4. Misses the importance of comprehensive evaluations of internal controls.
5. Does not provide specific guidance for an effective audit committee.
6. Encourages limited reporting of internal controls deficiencies.

The full text of Mr. Chapin's letter to COSO and the official reply of Robert L. May, Chairman, Committee of Sponsoring Organizations, and a memorandum from COSO, are included in the article "The COSO Report: Challenge and Counterchallenge," *Journal of Accountancy,* February 1993. The article was authored by Thomas P. Kelley, Group Vice-President, American Institute of CPAs, and his comments are included.

In June 1993, the AICPA requested the Securities and Exchange Commission to require management to report on its internal controls and for the outside auditor to assess those controls. The SEC has not been receptive to these recommendations now or in the past, although it may again review the recommendations.

The AICPA is one of the sponsoring organizations of COSO and a strong proponent of *Internal Control—Integrated Framework;* although a management report on internal controls may not be mandated soon, it probably will be recommended. Therefore, organizations should begin to initiate a review of internal controls as suggested in this chapter.

◄ HB ENTERPRISES ►

Chief Executive Office

SUBJECT: CUMULATIVE INDEX TO JANUARY 10, 1994

Retrieval Number	Date	Distribution	Subject
001	1/3/94	All Employees	Internal Control Policy/Procedure Statements
100	1/3/94	All Employees	Internal Control - Rights and Responsibilities
200	1/3/94	Designated	Glossary of Selected Terms
400	1/4/94	Senior Officers	Annual Report on Internal Control
500	1/3/94	Dept. Heads	Evaluation Tools - Control Environment
501	1/3/94	Dept. Heads	Evaluation Tools - Risk Assessment
502	1/3/94	Dept. Heads	Evaluation Tools - Control Activities
503	1/3/94	Dept. Heads	Evaluation Tools - Information and Communication
504	1/3/94	Dept. Heads	Evaluation Tools - Monitoring
505	1/4/94	Dept. Heads	Risk Assessment and Control Activities Worksheet
506	1/4/94	Dept. Heads	Overall Internal Control Systems Evaluation

Figure 3A.3. Typical policy/procedure index.

Internal Control Policy/Procedure

◄ HB ENTERPRISES ►

Chief Executive Office

SUBJECT: INTERNAL CONTROL POLICY/PROCEDURE STATEMENTS

To keep organization personnel informed of Company policy and major procedural changes related to the continuous review of internal control over operational, financial, and regulatory procedures and requirements, the Internal Control Policy/Procedure (ICP/P) system has been developed.

Such policies and procedures are not clerical processing procedures, job descriptions, or individual job task outlines, although they may contain some information on such items to fully understand the internal control problems and solutions.

Issuing an Internal Control Policy/Procedure

All ICP/Ps will be issued and controlled by the Office of the Chief Executive of the Company. However, any officer or employee may suggest a new Policy/Procedure by submitting a memorandum describing its content and purpose.

Printing and Distribution

The approved ICP/P will be duplicated on white paper, 3-hole punched, and corner-stapled if more than one page. Directors, Senior Officers, Department Heads, and Auditors will be provided ICP/P binders. New ICP/Ps should be communicated to employees whose actions may be affected. The manual should be available to all employees for reference.

Updating a Prior Internal Control Policy/Procedure

A new ICP/P must be issued if an existing one is to be modified in any way. The new ICP/P (with a new Retrieval No.) will indicate it supersedes the old ICP/P and the old one will be purged from the manual.

Index

A numerical index of all ICP/Ps will be issued as needed (Retrieval No. = INDEX). A copy will be sent to all employees with Manual binders.

Figure 3A.4. Initial internal control policy/procedure release.

Format

RETRIEVAL NO. — A 3-digit retrieval number (Series 001--999) will be assigned when the ICP/P is approved and issued. This number is located in the upper right hand corner on all pages.

PAGE — All pages (except attachments) will be numbered in the form Page 1 of 2. The page number will be located just below the Retrieval No. on all pages.

ISSUE DATE — Actual date the ICP/P was issued in the form "March 1, 1994."

DISTRIBUTION — The following distributions will be used depending on the contents of the ICP/P.

All employees	Department Heads	Senior Officers
Auditors	Designated	Supervisors
Board of Directors	Internal Auditors	Vice Presidents

The actual distribution of "Designated" will be listed at the end of the Statement. Specific Departments or employee names may be used.

SUPERSEDES — If the ICP/P supersedes a prior statement, the prior ICP/P Retrieval No. will be entered. Superseded items are purged from the Manual immediately.

SUBJECT — A short descriptive title of the Policy or Procedure (not to exceed one line) is used. The title will be used for indexing.

INTRODUCTION — Shown here will be a brief explanation of the background and/or purpose of the new ICP/P. If related to Administration or Board policy, a copy of the policy may be attached for reference.

PROCEDURE — The body includes a complete description of the policy and/or the procedure, the methods to be used, form names or attachments, and so forth. Most of the material in these policies and procedures will be taken from the four-volume series, Internal Control — Integrated Framework, of the Committee of Sponsoring Organizations of the Treadway Commission. The series was published September 1992.

ATTACHMENTS — Any attachments will be described, preferably by name of document and date such as "Board Minutes, January 1992" or name of form.

Attachment: Internal Control Policy/Procedure looseleaf binders

Distribution: Board of Directors, Senior Officers, Department Heads, Auditors

Figure 3A.4. Continued.

Internal Control Policy/Procedure

◄ HB ENTERPRISES ►

Chief Executive Office

- RETRIEVAL NO.   100
- PAGE   1 of 3
- ISSUE DATE   January 3, 1994
- DISTRIBUTION   All Employees
- SUPERSEDES

SUBJECT: INTERNAL CONTROL — ROLES AND RESPONSIBILITIES

Internal control systems operate at different levels of effectiveness. Internal control can be judged effective in each of three categories, respectively, if the board of directors and management have reasonable assurance that:

- They understand the extent to which the entity's objectives are being achieved.
- Published financial statements are being prepared reliably.
- Applicable laws and regulations are being complied with.

Internal control consists of five interrelated components.

Control Environment — The control environment sets the tone of an organization, influencing the control consciousness of its people. Control environment factors include the integrity, ethical values and competence of the entity's people; management's philosophy and operating style; the way management assigns authority and responsibility, and organizes and develops its people; and the attention and direction provided by the board of directors.

Risk Assessment — Every entity faces a variety of risks from external and internal sources that must be assessed. . . . Risk assessment is the identification and analysis of relevant risks to achievement of the objectives, forming a basis for determining how the risks should be managed. Because economic, industry, regulatory and operating conditions will continue to change, mechanisms are needed to identify and deal with the special risks associated with change.

Control Activities — Control activities are the policies and procedures that help ensure management directives are carried out. . . . Control activities occur throughout the organization, at all levels and in all functions. They include a range of activities as diverse as approvals, authorizations, verifications, reconciliations, reviews of operating performance, security of assets and segregation of duties.

Information and Communication — Pertinent information must be identified, captured and communicated in a form and time frame that enables people to carry out their resonsibilities. . . . All personnel must receive a clear message from top management that control responsibilities must be taken seriously. They must understand their own role in the internal control system, as well as how individual activities relate to the work of others. They must have a means of communicating significant

Figure 3A.5.   Internal control—roles and responsibilities release.

information upstream. There also needs to be effective communication with external parties, such as customers, suppliers, regulators and shareholders.

Monitoring — Internal control systems need to be monitored — a process that assesses the quality of the system's performance over time. This is accomplished through ongoing monitoring activities, separate evaluations or a combination of the two. . . . The scope and frequency of separate evaluations will depend primarily on an assessment of risks and the effectiveness of ongoing monitoring procedures. Internal control deficiencies should be reported upstream, with serious matters reported to top management and the board.

What Internal Control Can Do

Internal control can help an entity achieve its performance and profitability targets, and prevent loss of resources. It can help ensure reliable financial reporting. And it can help ensure that the enterprise complies with laws and regulations, avoiding damage to its reputation and other consequences.

What Internal Control Cannot Do

Internal control can(not) ensure an entity's success — that is, ensure achievement of basic business objectives or ensure survival. Even effective internal control can only help an entity achieve these objectives. Internal control cannot change an inherently poor manager into a good one, . . . and cannot ensure success, or even survival.

(The belief that) internal control can ensure the reliability of financial reporting and compliance with laws and regulations is also unwarranted. An internal control system, no matter how well conceived and operated, can provide only reasonable — not absolute — assurance to management and the board regarding achievement of an entity's objectives. The likelihood of achievment is affected by limitations inherent in all internal control systems. These include the realities that judgments in decision-making can be faulty, and that breakdowns can occur because of simple error or mistake. Additionally, controls can be circumvented by the collusion of two or more people, and management has the ability to override the system. Another limiting factor is that the design of an internal control system must reflect the fact that there are resource constraints, and the benefits of controls must be considered relative to their costs.

Roles and Responsibilities

Everyone in an organization has responsibility for internal control.

Management — The chief executive officer is ultimately responsible and should assume "ownership" of the system. More than any other individual, the chief executive sets the "tone at the top" that affects integrity and ethics and other factors of a positive control environment. At HB Enterprises, the Chief Executive fulfills this duty by providing leadership and direction to senior managers and reviewing the way they're controlling the business. Senior

Figure 3A.5. Continued.

managers, in turn, assign responsibility for establishment of more specific internal control policies and procedures to personnel responsible for the unit's functions. In any event, in a cascading responsiblity, a manager is effectively a chief executive of his or her sphere of responsibility. Of particular significance are financial officers and their staffs, whose control activities cut across, as well as up and down, the operating and other units of an enterprise.

Board of Directors — Management is accountable to the board of directors, which provides governance, guidance, and oversight. Effective board members are objective, capable and inquisitive. They also have a knowledge of the entity's activities and environment, and commit the time necessary to fulfill their board responsibilities. . . . A strong, active board, particularly when coupled with effective upward communications channels and capable financial, legal and internal audit functions, is often best able to identify and correct such a problem.

Internal Auditors — Internal auditors play an important role in evaluating the effectiveness of control systems, and contribute to ongoing effectiveness. Because of organizational position and authority in an entity, an internal audit function often plays a significant monitoring role.

Other Personnel — Internal control is, to some degree, the responsibility of everyone in an organization and therefore should be an explicit or implicit part of everyone's job description. Virtually all employees produce information used in the internal control system or take other actions needed to effect control. Also, all personnel should be responsible for communicating upward problems in operations, noncompliance with the code of conduct, or other policy violations or illegal actions.

A number of external parties often contribute to achievement of an entity's objectives. External auditors, bringing an independent and objective view, contribute directly through the financial statement audit and indirectly by providing information useful to management and the board of directors in carrying out their responsibilities. Others providing information to the entity useful in effecting internal control are legislators and regulators, customers and others transacting business with the enterprise, financial analysts, bond raters and the news media. External parties, however, are not responsible for, or are they a part of, the entity's internal control system.

Figure 3A.5. Continued.

Internal Control Policy/Procedure

◄ HB ENTERPRISES ►

Chief Executive Office

- RETRIEVAL NO.   200
- PAGE   1 of 4
- ISSUE DATE   January 3, 1994
- DISTRIBUTION   Designated
- SUPERSEDES

SUBJECT: GLOSSARY OF SELECTED TERMS

Application Controls—Programmed procedures in application software, and related manual procedures, designed to help ensure the completeness and accuracy of information processing. Examples include computerized edit checks of input data, numerical sequence checks, and manual procedures to follow up on items listed in exception reports.

Category—One of three groupings of objectives of internal control, control activities, or controls. The categories are effectiveness and efficiency of operations, reliability of financial reporting, and compliance with applicable laws and regulations. The categories overlap, so that a particular objective, for example, might fall into more than one category.

Compliance—Having to do with conforming with laws and regulations applicable to an entity.

Component—One of five elements of internal control. The internal control components are the control environment, risk assessment, control activities, information and communication, and monitoring.

Computer Controls—(1) Controls performed by computer, that is, controls programmed into computer software (contrast with **Manual Controls**). (2) Controls over computer processing of information, consisting of general controls and application controls (both programmed and manual).

Control—(1) A noun, used as a subject, for example, existence of a control—a policy or procedure that is part of internal control. A control can exist within any of the five components. (2) A noun, used as an object, for example, to effect control—the result of policies and procedures designed to control; this result may or may not be effective internal control. (3) A verb, for example, to control—to regulate; to establish or implement a policy that effects control.

Criteria—A set of standards against which an internal control system can be measured in determining effectiveness. The five internal control components, taken in the context of inherent limitations of internal control, represent criteria for internal control effectiveness for each of the three control categories. For one category, reliability of financial reporting, there is a more detailed criterion, the material weakness concept.

Deficiency—A perceived, potential or real internal control shortcoming, or an opportunity to strengthen the internal control system to provide a greater likelihood that the entity's objectives are achieved.

Figure 3A.6. Internal control glossary.

Design—(1) Intent. As used in the definition of internal control, the internal control system design is intended to provide reasonable assurance as to achievement of objectives; when the intent is realized, the system can be deemed effective. (2) Plan; the way a system is supposed to work, contrasted with how it actually works.

Detective Control—a control designed to discover an unintended event or result (contrast with **Preventive Control**).

Effected—Used with an internal control system: devised and maintained.

Effective Internal Control—Internal control can be judged effective in each of the three categories, respectively, if the board of directors and management have reasonable assurance that:
- They understand the extent to which the entity's operations objectives are being achieved.
- Published financial statements are being prepared reliably.
- Applicable laws and regulations are being complied with.

Effective Internal Control System—A synonym for **Effective Internal Control**.

Entity—An organization of any size established for a particular purpose. An entity may, for example, be a business enterprise, not-for-profit organization, government body, or academic institution. Other terms used as synonyms include organization and enterprise.

Ethical Values—Moral values that enable a decision maker to determine an appropriate course of behavior; these values should be based on what is "right," which may go beyond what is "legal."

Financial Reporting—Used with "objectives" or "controls": having to do with the reliability of **published financial statements**.

General Controls—Policies and procedures that help ensure the continued, proper operation of computer information systems. They include controls over data center operations, system software acquisition and maintenance, access security, and application system development and maintenance. General controls support the functioning of programmed application controls. Other terms sometimes used to describe general controls are general computer controls and information technology controls.

Inherent Limitations—Those limitations of all internal control systems. The limitations relate to the limits of human judgment; resource constraints and the need to consider the cost of controls in relation to expected benefits; the reality that breakdowns can occur; and the possibility of management override and collusion.

Integrity—The quality or state of being of sound moral principle; uprightness, honesty, and sincerity; the desire to do the right thing, to profess and live up to a set of values and expectations.

Figure 3A.6. Continued.

Internal Control—A process, effected by an entity's board of directors, management, and other personnel, designed to provide reasonable assurance regarding the achievement of objectives in the following categories:

- Effectiveness and efficiency of operations.
- Reliability of financial reporting.
- Compliance with applicable laws and regulations.

When an internal control system satisfies specified criteria, it can be deemed effective.

Internal Control System—A synonym for **Internal Control**.

Management Controls—Controls performed by one or more managers at any level in an organization.

Management Intervention—Management's actions to overrule prescribed policies or procedures for legitimate purposes; management intervention is usually necessary to deal with non-recurring and non-standard transactions or events that otherwise might be handled inappropriately by the system (contrast this term with **Management Override**).

Management Override—Management's overruling of prescribed policies or procedures for illegitimate purposes with the intent of personal gain or an enhanced presentation of an entity's financial condition or compliance status (contrast this term with **Management Intervention**).

Management Process—The series of actions taken by management to run an entity. An internal control system is a part of and integrated with the management process.

Manual Controls—Controls performed manually, not by computer (contrast with **Computer Controls** (1)).

Operations—Used with "objectives" or "controls": having to do with the effectiveness or efficiency of an entity's operations, including performance and profitability goals, and safeguarding resources.

Policy—Management's dictate of what should be done to effect control. A policy serves as the basis for procedures for its implementation.

Preventive Control—A control designed to avoid an unintended event or result (contrast with **Detective Control**).

Procedure—An action that implements a policy.

Published Financial Statements—Financial statements, interim and condensed financial statements, and selected data derived from such statements, such as earnings releases, reported publicly.

Figure 3A.6. Continued.

23

Reasonable Assurance—The concept that internal control, no matter how well designed and operated, cannot guarantee that an entity's objectives will be met. This is because of **Inherent Limitations** in all internal control systems.

Reliability of Financial Reporting—Used in the context of **published financial statements**, reliability is defined as the preparation of financial statements fairly presented in conformity with generally accepted (or other relevant and appropriate) accounting principles and regulatory requirements for external purposes, within the context of materiality. Supporting fair presentation are the five basic financial statement assertions: existence or occurrence, completeness, rights and obligations, valuation or allocation, and presentation and disclosure. When applied to interim or condensed financial statements or selected data derived from such statements, the factors representing fair presentation and the assertions apply only to the extent they are relevant to the presentation.

Reportable Condition—An internal control deficiency related to financial reporting; it is a significant deficiency in the design or operation of the internal control system, which could adversely affect the entity's ability to record, process, summarize, and report financial data consistent with the assertions of management in the financial statements.

Distribution: Board of Directors
                 Senior Officers
                 Department Heads

Figure 3A.6. Continued.

Internal Control Policy/Procedure

◄ HB ENTERPRISES ►

Chief Executive Office

· RETRIEVAL NO. 400
·
· PAGE   1 of 3
·
· ISSUE DATE   January 4, 1994
·
· DISTRIBUTION   Senior Officers
·
· SUPERSEDES

SUBJECT: ANNUAL REPORT ON INTERNAL CONTROL

The Board of Directors and Senior Officers have met several times to discuss whether HB Enterprises should include a separate section to report on the Company's internal control in the annual published report to stockholders and others. It has been decided that such a report would be included for this fiscal year ending December 31, 1994.

The report to external parties will concern itself primarily with controls over only the annual financial reporting. As stated in Internal Control - Integrated Framework:

> **Differentiating Control Categories**. Because there is overlap among objectives, it can be difficult to determine which controls are within the scope of a report dealing with controls over financial reporting. Despite this difficulty, it is important to set boundaries to ensure that reasonable expectations of report users are matched with the reality of the report's scope. . . .
>
> . . . two concepts should be kept in mind:
>
> First, in most internal control systems, controls often serve to accomplish more than one objective. Frequently, controls established primarily to accomplish operations or compliance objectives may also accomplish financial reporting objectives. In those instances, where traditional financial reporting controls are not present, management may be able to look to other controls that serve the same purpose. . .
>
> Second, controls directed at operations or compliance may deal with events, transactions or other occurrences that must be reported in the entity's financial statements. This does not mean that operations and compliance controls fall within the scope of the management report. Rather, results of the activities subject to those other controls must be properly reflected in the financial statements.
>
> **Discussion of Specific Elements**. A discussion of specific elements of the entity's internal control system has been suggested in recommendations put forth by varous individuals and groups. Specific areas addressed in reports published to date vary, but the focus generally is on some or all of the following items.
>
> - **Audit Committee** - The composition and role of the entity's audit committee is frequently a part of the discussion of internal control. This discussion may emphasize the audit committee's role and describe its duties.

Figure 3A.7. Statement on annual report on internal control.

- **Establishing and Communicating Written Policies** - Some published reports contain a statement that management has established written internal control policies and procedures consistent with the objectives of internal control. Reports often state that management regularly communicates these policies and procedures to employees.

- **Organizational Relationships** - Published reports sometimes recognize the significance of the delegation of authority and segregation of responsibility to effective internal control. This recognition might be given through a statement that the internal control system provides for appropriate reporting relationships and division of responsibility.

- **Personnel** - Published reports sometimes address the careful selection and training of personnel and may also mention recruiting and development. The statements are made with respect to personnel or staff in general, or to financial or operating personnel or managers in particular.

- **Code of Conduct** - A number of published reports discuss an entity's code of conduct. The discussion may encompass communication of the code's provisions; the major subjects addressed in the code . . . ; and existence of a systematic program to assess compliance with the code.

- **Program of Internal Auditing** - Many reports refer to the entity's program of internal auditing. These references are usually limited to a statement that the entity maintains an effective (or strong or comprehensive) internal auditing program that independently assesses the effectiveness of the internal control system and recommends potential improvements in it.

Management report content should include:

- The category of controls being addressed (. . . published financial statements).

- A statement about the inherent limitations of internal control systems.

- A statement about the existence of mechanisms for system monitoring and responding to identified control deficiencies.

- A frame of reference for reporting - that is, identification of the criteria against which the internal control system is measured.

- A conclusion on the effectiveness of the internal control system. If one or more material weaknesses exist, which would preclude a statement that the criteria for system effectiveness are met, a description of the material weaknesses should be included.

- The date as of which (or the period for which) the conclusion is made.

- The names of the report signers.

Figure 3A.7. Continued.

An illustrative report that conforms to these guidelines and uses the criteria contained in this report is as follows:

> XYZ Company maintains a system of internal control over financial reporting, which is designed to provide reasonable assurance to the Company's management and board of directors regarding the preparation of reliable published financial statements. The system contains self-monitoring mechanisms, and actions are taken to correct deficiencies as they are identified. Even an effective internal control system, no matter how well designed, has inherent limitations—including the possibility of the circumvention or overriding of controls—and therefore can provide only reasonable assurance with respect to financial statement preparation. Further, because of changes in conditions, internal control system effectiveness may vary over time.
>
> The Company assessed its internal control system as of December 31, 19XX in relation to criteria for effective internal control over financial reporting, described in "Internal Control—Integrated Framework" issued by the Committee of Sponsoring Organization of the Treadway Commission. Based on this assessment, the Company believes that, as of December 31, 19XX, its system of internal control over financial reporting met those criteria.
>
> XYZ Company
>
> by_____
>   Signature (CEO)
>
> _____   by_____
> Date   Signature(CFO/Chief Accounting Officer)

The Auditing Standards Board of the American Institute of Certified Public Accountants has approved the Statement on Standards for Attestation Engagements - No. 2, "Reporting on an Entity's Internal Control Structure Over Financial Reporting." The statement was effective when the assertion is as of December 15, 1993 or thereafter. HB Enterprises will not ask for an independent attestation as of December 31, 1994, but may do so for later years.

Action. Internal Audit, beginning now and continuing to early fall, will be interviewing all department heads to develop a commprehensive program of examination of internal control related to the preparation of annual financial statements. During the last three months of the fiscal year, the internal control reviews will completed, with cooperation of the departments involved and the independent auditors.

Portions reprinted with permission from *Internal Control—Integrated Framework*, Copyright © 1992 by the Committee of Sponsoring Organizations of the Treadway Commission.

Figure 3A.7. Continued.

Internal Control Policy/Procedure

◄ HB ENTERPRISES ►

Chief Executive Office

SUBJECT: EVALUATION TOOLS - CONTROL ENVIRONMENT

Five evaluation tools are presented, one for each internal control component. These components are Control Environment, Risk Assessment, Control Activities, Information and Communication, and Monitoring. This statement covers Control Environment.

These evaluation tools are intended to provide guidance and assistance in evaluating internal control systems in relation to criteria for effective internal control set forth in the Framework volume.

These tools are presented for *purely illustrative* purposes, and their presentation here *in no way* suggests that all matters addressed in them need to be considered in evaluating an internal control system, or that all such matters must be present in order to conclude that a system is effective. We may use different evaluation tools, or use other methodologies utilizing different evaluative techniques.

Included under each point of focus (in bolf type) are examples of subsidiary issues that might be considered in addressing the point of focus. It is important to recognize that only a *few* examples of such subsidiary issues are provided. Many others usually are relevant. The examples provided are intended only to illustrate the *types* of items to consider.

The evaluator addresses each point of focus, considering the example subsidiary issues as well as others not presented. Although one could record a response for each example subsidiary issue, it is suggested that a response be provided only to the point of focus. The forms to be used will include a "description/comments" column to provide space to record a description of how matters addressed in the point of focus are applied in the entity, and to record relevant comments. The response generally will not be a "yes" or "no" answer, but rather information on how the entity addresses the matter.

EVALUATION FORM   AREA OF STUDY_____

POINTS OF FOCUS	DESCRIPTION/COMMENTS
(Description of points to be considered)	(Evaluator's study comments)

At the end of each section is a space to record a conclusion on the effectiveness of the related controls, and any actions that might need to be taken or considered. Space is provided at the end of each tool for similar information on the entire component.

Figure 3A.8.   Statement on evaluation tools—control environment.

Control Environment - Points of Focus

Integrity and Ethical Values

Management must convey the message that integrity and ethical values cannot be compromised, and employees must receive and understand that message. Management must continually demonstrate, through words and actions, a commitment to high ethical standards.

Existence and implementation of codes of conduct and other policies regarding acceptable business practice, conflicts of interest, or expected standards of ethical and moral behavior. For example, consider whether:

1. Codes are comprehensive, addressing conflicts of interest, illegal or other improper payments, anti-competitive guidelines, insider trading.

2. Codes are periodically acknowledged by all employees.

3. Employees understand what behavior is acceptable or unacceptable, and know what to do if they encounter improper behavior.

4. If a written code of conduct does not exist, the management culture emphasizes the importance of integrity and ethical behavior. This may be communicated orally in staff meetings, in one-on-one interface, or by example when dealing with day-to-day activities.

Establishment of the "tone at the top"--including explicit moral guidance about what is right and wrong--and extent of its communication throughout the organization. For example, consider whether:

1. Commitment to integrity and ethics is communicated effectively throughout the enterprise, both in words and deeds.

2. Employees feel peer pressure to do the right thing, or cut corners to make a "quick buck."

3. Management appropriately deals with signs that problems exist, e.g., potential defective products or hazardous wastes, especially when the cost of identifying problems and dealing with the issues could be large.

Dealings with employees, suppliers, customers, investors, creditors, insurers, competitors, and auditors, etc. (e.g., whether management conducts business on a high ethical plane, and insists that others do so, or pays little attention to ethical issues). For example, consider whether:

Figure 3A.8. Continued.

29

1. Everyday dealings with customers, suppliers, employees and other parties are based on honesty and fairness (e.g., customer's overpayment or a supplier's underbilling are not ignored, no efforts are made to find a way to reject an employee's legitimate claim for benefits, and reports to lenders are complete, accurate and not misleading).

Appropriateness of remedial action taken in response to departures from approved policies and procedures or violations of the code of conduct. Extent to which remedial action is communicated or otherwise becomes known throughout the entity. For example, consider whether:

1. Management responds to violations of behavioral standards.

2. Disciplinary actions taken as a result of violations are widely communicated in the entity. Employees believe that, if caught violating behavioral standards, they'll suffer the consequences.

Management's attitude towards intervention or overriding established controls. For example, consider whether:

1. Management has provided guidance on the situations and frequency with which intervention may be needed.

2. Management intervention is documented and explained appropriately.

3. Manager override is explicitly prohibited.

4. Deviations from established policies are investigated and documented.

Pressure to meet unrealistic performance targets--particularly for short-term results--and extent to which compensation is based on achieving those performance targets. For example, consider whether:

1. Conditions such as extreme incentives or temptations exist that can unnecessarily and unfairly test people's adherence to ethical values.

2. Compensation and promotions are based solely on achievement of short-term performance targets.

3. Controls are in place to reduce temptations that might otherwise exist.

Conclusions/Actions Needed

Figure 3A.8. Continued.

Commitment to Competence

Management must specify the level of competence needed for particular jobs, and translate the desired levels of competence into requisite knowledge and skills.

Formal or informal job descriptions or other means of defining tasks that comprise particular jobs. For example, consider whether:

1. Management has analyzed, on a formal or informal basis, the tasks comprising particular jobs, considering such factors as the extent to which individuals must exercise judgment and the extent of related supervision.

Analyses of the knowledge and skills needed to perform jobs adequately. For example, consider whether:

1. Management has determined to an adequate extent the knowledge and skills needed to perform particular jobs.

2. Evidence exists indicating that employees appear to have the requisite knowledge and skills.

Conclusions/Actions Needed

Board of Directors or Audit Committee

An active and effective board, or committees thereof, provides an important oversight function and, because of management's ability to override system controls, the board plays an important role in ensuring effective internal control.

Independence from management, such that necessary, even if difficult and probing, questions are raised. For example, consider whether:

1. The board constructively challenges management's planned decisions, e.g., strategic initiatives and major transactions, and probes for explanations of past results (e.g., budget variances).

2. A board that consists solely of an entity's officers and employees (e.g., a small corporation) questions and scrutinizes activities, presents alternative views and takes appropriate action if necessary.

Figure 3A.8. Continued.

Use of board committees where warranted by the need for more in-depth or directed attention to particular matters. For example, consider whether:

1. Board committees exist.

2. They are sufficient, in subject matter and membership, to deal with important issues adequately.

Knowledge and experience of directors. For example, consider whether:

1. Directors have sufficient knowledge, industry experience and time to serve effectively.

Frequency and timeliness with which meetings are held with chief financial and/or accounting officers, internal auditors and external auditors. For example, consider whether:

1. The audit committee meets privately with the chief accounting officer and internal and external auditors to discuss the reasonableness of the financial reporting process, system of internal control, significant comments and recommendations, and management's performance.

2. The audit committee reviews the scope of activities of the internal and external auditors annually.

Sufficiency and timeliness with which information is provided to board or committee members, to allow monitoring of management's objectives and strategies, the entity's financial position and operating results, and terms of significant agreements. For example, consider whether:

1. The board regularly receives key information, such as financial statements, major marketing initiatives, significant contracts or negotiations.

2. Directors believe they receive the proper information.

Sufficiency and timeliness with which the board or audit committee is apprised of sensitive information, investigations and improper acts (e.g., travel expenses of senior officers, significant litigation, investigations of regulatory agencies, defalcations, embezzlement or misuse of corporate assets, violations of insider trading rules, political payments, illegal payments). For example, consider whether:

1. A process exists for informing the board of significant issues.

2. Information is communicated timely.

Figure 3A.8. Continued.

Oversight in determining the compensation of executive officers and head of internal audit, and the appointment and termination of those individuals. For example, consider whether:

1. The compensation committee approves all management incentive plans tied to performance.

2. The compensation committee, in joint consultation with the audit committee, deals with compensation and retention issues regarding the chief internal auditor.

Role in establishing the appropriate "tone at the top." For example, consider whether:

1. The board and audit committee are involved sufficiently in evaluating the effectiveness of the "tone at the top."

2. The board takes steps to ensure an appropriate "tone."

3. The board specifically addresses management's adherence to the code of conduct.

Actions the board or committee takes as a result of its findings, including special investigations as needed. For example, consider whether:

1. The board has issued directives to management detailing specific actions to be taken.

2. The board oversees and follows up as needed.

Conclusions/Actions Needed

Management's Philosophy and Operating Style

The philosophy and operating style of management normally have a pervasive effect on an entity. These are, of course, intangibles, but one can look for positive or negative signs.

Nature of business risks accepted, e.g., whether management often enters into particularly high-risk ventures, or is extremely conservative in accepting risks. For example, consider whether:

1. Management moves carefully, proceeding only after carefully analyzing the risks and potential benefits of a venture.

Figure 3A.8. Continued.

33

Personnel turnover in key functions, e.g., operating, accounting, data processing, internal audit. For example, consider whether:

1. There has been excessive turnover of management or supervisory personnel.

2. Key personnel have quit unexpectedly or on short notice.

3. There is a pattern to turnover (e.g., inability to retain key financial or internal audit executives) that may be an indicator of the emphasis that management places on control.

Management's attitude toward the data processing and accounting functions, and concerns about the reliability of financial reporting and safeguarding of assets. For example, consider whether:

1. The accounting function is viewed as a necessary group of "bean counters," or as a vehicle for exercising control over the entity's various activities.

2. The selection of accounting principles used in financial statements always results in the highest reported income.

3. If the accounting function is decentralized, operating management "sign off" on reported results.

4. Unit accounting personnel also have responsibility to central financial officers.

5. Valuable assets, including intellectual assets and information, are protected from unauthorized access or use.

Frequency of interaction between senior management and operating management, particularly when operating from geographically removed locations. For example, consider whether:

1. Senior managers frequently visit subsidiary or divisional operations.

2. Group or divisional management meetings are held frequently.

Attitudes and actions toward financial reporting, including disputes over application of accounting treatments (e.g., selection of conservative versus liberal accounting policies; whether accounting principles have been misapplied, important financial information not disclosed, or records manipulated or falsified). For example, consider whether:

1. Management avoids obsessive focus on short-term reported results.

Figure 3A.8. Continued.

2. Personnel do not submit inappropriate reports to meet targets (e.g., salespeople submitting orders to meet targets, knowing customers will return goods in the next period).

3. Managers do not ignore signs of inappropriate practices.

4. Estimates do not stretch facts to the edge of reasonableness and beyond.

Conclusions/Actions Needed

Organizational Structure

The organizational structure shouldn't be so simple that it cannot adequately monitor the enterprise's activities nor so complex that it inhibits the necessary flow of information. Executives should fully understand their control responsibilities and possess the requisite experience and levels of knowledge commensurate with their positions.

Appropriateness of the entity's organizational structure, and its ability to provide the necessary information flow to manage its activities. For example, consider whether:

1. The organizational structure is appropriately centralized or decentralized, given the nature of the entity's operations.

2. The structure facilitates the flow of information upstream, downstream and across all business activities.

Adequacy of definition of key managers' responsibilities, and their understanding of these responsibilities. For example, consider whether:

1. Responsibilities and expectations for the entity's business activities are communicated clearly to the executives in charge of those activities.

Adequacy of knowledge and experience of key managers in light of responsibilities. For example, consider whether:

1. The executives in charge have the required knowledge, experience and training to perform their duties.

Appropriateness of reporting relationships. For example, consider whether:

1. Established reporting relationships--formal or informal, direct or matrix--are effective, and they provide managers information appropriate to their responsibilities and authority.

Figure 3A.8. Continued.

35

2. The executives of the business activities have access to communication channels to senior operating executives.

Extent to which modifications to the organizational structure are made in light of changed conditions. For example, consider whether:

1. Management periodically evaluates the entity's organizational structure in light of changes in the business or industry.

Sufficient numbers of employees exist, particularly in management and supervisory capacities. For example, consider whether:

1. Managers and supervisors have sufficient time to carry out their responsibilities effectively.

2. Managers and supervisors work excessive overtime, and are fulfilling the responsibilities of more than one employee.

Conclusions/Actions Needed

Assignment of Authority and Responsibility

The assignment of responsibility, delegation of authority and establishment of related policies provide a basis for accountability and control, and set forth individuals' respective roles.

Assignment of responsibility and delegation of authority to deal with organizational goals and objectives, operating functions and regulatory requirements, including responsibility for information systems and authorizations for changes. For example, consider whether:

1. Authority and responsibility are assigned to employees throughout the entity.

2. Responsibility for decisions is related to assignment of authority and responsibility.

3. Proper information is considered in determining the level of authority and scope of responsibility assigned to an individual.

Appropriateness of control-related standards and procedures, including employee job descriptions. For example, consider whether:

1. Job descriptions, for at least management and supervisory personnel, exist.

Figure 3A.8. Continued.

2. They contain specific references to control-related responsibilities.

Appropriate numbers of people, particularly with respect to data processing and accounting functions, with the requisite skill levels relative to the size of the entity and nature and complexity of activities and systems. For example, consider whether:

1. The entity has an adequate workforce--in numbers and experience--to carry out its mission.

Appropriateness of delegated authority in relation to assigned responsibilities. For example, consider whether:

1. There is an appropriate balance between authority needed to "get the job done" and the involvement of senior personnel where needed.

2. Employees at the "right" level are empowered to correct problems or implement improvements, and empowerment is accompanied by appropriate levels of competence and clear boundaries of authority.

Conclusions/Actions Needed

HUMAN RESOURCE POLICIES AND PRACTICES

Human resource policies are central to recruiting and retaining competent people to enable the entity's plans to be carried out so its goals can be achieved.

Extent to which policies and procedures for hiring, training, promoting and compensating employees are in place. For example, consider whether:

1. Existing personnel policies and procedures result in recruiting or developing competent and trustworthy people necessary to support an effective internal control system.

2. The level of attention given to recruiting and training the right people is appropriate.

3. When formal documentation of policies and practices does not exist, management communicates expectations about the type of people to be hired or participates directly in the hiring process.

Extent to which people are made aware of their responsibilities and expectations of them. For example, consider whether:

1. New employees are made aware of their responsibilities and management's expectations.

Figure 3A.8. Continued.

37

2. Supervisory personnel meet periodically with employees to review job performance and suggestions for improvement.

Appropriateness of remedial action taken in response to departures from approved policies and procedures. For example, consider whether:

1. Management's response to failures to carry out assigned responsibilities is appropriate.

2. Appropriate corrective action is taken as a result of non-adherence to established policies.

3. Employees understand that ineffective performance will result in remedial consequences.

Extent to which personnel policies address adherence to appropriate ethical and moral standards. For example, consider whether:

1. Integrity and ethical values is a criterion in performance appraisals.

Adequacy of employee candidate background checks, particularly with regard to prior actions or activities considered to be unacceptable by the entity. For example, consider whether:

1. Candidates with frequent job changes or gaps in employment history are subjected to particularly close scrutiny.

2. Hiring policies require investigation for a criminal record.

Adequacy of employee retention and promotion criteria and information-gathering techniques (e.g., performance evaluations) and relation to the code of conduct or other behavioral guidelines. For example, consider whether:

1. Promotion and salary increase criteria are detailed clearly so that individuals know what management expects prior to promotions or advancement.

2. Criteria reflect adherence to behavioral standards.

Conclusions/Actions Needed

Component Summary--Conclusions/Actions Needed

Figure 3A.8. Continued.

◄ HB ENTERPRISES ►

Chief Executive Office

- RETRIEVAL NO.   501
- PAGE   1 of 9
- ISSUE DATE   January 3, 1994
- DISTRIBUTION   Dept. Heads
- SUPERSEDES

SUBJECT: EVALUATION TOOLS - RISK ASSESSMENT

The five internal control components are Control Environment, Risk Assessment, Control Activities, Information and Communication, and Monitoring. This statement covers the evaluation tools for the Risk assessment component.

These evaluation tools are intended to provide guidance and assistance in evaluating internal control systems in relation to criteria for effective internal control set forth in the "Framework" volume of <u>Internal Control—Integrated Framework</u>.

These tools are presented for *purely illustrative* purposes, and their presentation here *in no way* suggests that all matters addressed in them need to be considered in evaluating an internal control system, or that all such matters must be present in order to conclude that a system is effective. We may use different evaluation tools, or use other methodologies utilizing different evaluative techniques.

Included under each point of focus (in bold type) are examples of subsidiary issues that might be considered in addressing the point of focus. It is important to recognize that only a *few* examples of such subsidiary issues are provided. Many others usually are relevant. The examples provided are intended only to illustrate the *types* of items to consider.

The evaluator addresses each point of focus, considering the example subsidiary issues as well as others not presented. Although one could record a response for each example subsidiary issue, it is suggested that a response be provided only to the point of focus. The forms to be used will include a "description/comments" column to provide space to record a description of how matters addressed in the point of focus are applied in the entity, and to record relevant comments. The response generally will not be a "yes" or "no" answer, but rather information on how the entity addresses the matter. Following is the Evaluation Form layout:

EVALUATION FORM   AREA OF STUDY_____

POINTS OF FOCUS	DESCRIPTION/COMMENTS
(Description of points to be considered)	(Evaluator's study comments)

At the end of each section is a space to record a conclusion on the effectiveness of the related controls, and any actions that might need to be taken or considered. Space is provided at the end of each tool for similar information on the entire component.

Figure 3A.9.   Statement on evaluation tools—risk assessment.

RISK ASSESSMENT - POINTS OF FOCUS

Entity-Wide Objectives

For an entity to have effective control, it must have established objectives. Entity-wide objectives include broad statements of what an entity desires to achieve, and are supported by related strategic plans. Describe the entity-wide objectives and key strategies that have been established.

Extent to which the entity-wide objectives provide sufficiently broad statements and guidance on what the entity desires to achieve, yet which are specific enough to relate directly to this entity. For example, consider whether:

1. Management has established entity-wide objectives.

2. The entity-wide objectives are different than generic objectives that could apply to any entity (e.g., generate sufficient cash flow to service debt, or produce a reasonable return on investment).

Effectiveness with which the entity-wide objectives are communicated to employees and board of directors. For example, consider whether:

1. Information on the entity-wide objectives is disseminated to employees and the board of directors.

2. Management obtains feedback from key managers, other employees and the board signifying that communication to employees is effective.

Relation and consistency of strategies with entity-wide objectives. For example, consider whether:

1. The strategic plan supports the entity-wide objectives.

2. It addresses high level resource allocations and priorities.

Consistency of business plans and budgets with entity-wide objectives, strategic plans and current conditions. For example, consider whether:

1. Assumptions inherent in the plans and budgets reflect the entity's historical experience and current conditions.

2. Plans and budgets are at an appropriate level of detail for each management level.

Figure 3A.9. Continued.

Conclusions/Actions Needed

Activity-Level Objectives

Activity-level objectives flow from and are linked with the entity-wide objectives and strategies. Activity-level objectives are frequently stated as goals with specific targets and deadlines. Objectives should be established for each significant activity, and those activity-level objectives should be consistent with each other.

Linkage of activity-level objectives with entity-wide objectives and strategic plans. For example, consider whether:

1. Adequate linkage exists for all significant activities.

2. Activity-level objectives are reviewed from time to time for continued relevance.

Consistency of activity-level objectives with each other. For example, consider whether:

1. They are complementary and reinforcing within activities.

2. They are complementary and reinforcing between activities.

Relevance of activity-level objectives to all significant business processes. For example, consider whether:

1. Objectives are established for key activities in the flows of goods and services and support activities.

2. Activity-level objectives are consistent with past practices and performances or with industry or functional analogues, or the reasons for variance have been considered.

3. Objectives are established for each significant activity. These activities may include, among others:

> Inbound
> Operations
> Outbound
> Marketing and Sales
> Service
> Procurement
> Technology Development

Figure 3A.9. Continued.

Human Resources
Manage the Enterprise
Manage External Relations
Provide Administrative Services
Manage Information Technology
Manage Risks (of accident or other insurable loss)
Manage Legal Affairs
Plan
Process Accounts Payable
Process Accounts Receivable
Process Funds
Process Fixed Assets
Analyze and Reconcile
Process Benefits and Retiree Information
Process Payroll
Process Tax Compliance
Process Product Costs
Provide Financial and Management Reporting

Specificity of activity-level objectives. For example, consider whether:

1. Objectives include measurement criteria.

Adequacy of resources relative to objectives. For example, consider whether:

1. Management has identified the resources needed to achieve the objectives.

2. Plans exist for acquiring necessary resources (e.g., financing, personnel, facilities, technology).

Identification of objectives that are important (critical success factors) to achievement of entity-wide objectives. For example, consider whether:

1. Management has identified what must go right, or where failure must be avoided, for entity-wide objectives to be achieved.

2. Capital spending and expense budgets are based on management's analysis of the relative importance of objectives.

3. The objectives serving as critical success factors provide a basis for particular management focus.

Figure 3A.9. Continued.

Involvement of all levels of management in objective setting and extent to which they are committed to the objectives. For example, consider whether:

1. Managers participate in establishing activity objectives for which they are responsible.

2. Procedures exist to resolve disagreements.

3. Managers support the objectives, and do not have "hidden agendas."

Conclusions/Actions Needed

Risks

An entity's risk-assessment process should identify and consider the implications of relevant risks, at both the entity level and the activity level. The risk-assessment process should consider external and internal factors that could impact achievement of the objectives, should analyze the risks, and provide a basis for managing them.

Adequacy of mechanisms to identify risks arising from external sources. For example, consider whether management considers risks related to:

> Supply sources
> Technology changes
> Creditor's demands
> Competitor's actions
> Economic conditions
> Political conditions
> Regulation
> Natural events

Adequacy of mechanisms to identify risks arising from internal sources. For example, consider whether management considers risks related to:

1. Human resources, such as retention of key management personnel or changes in responsibilities that can affect the ability to function effectively.

2. Financing, such as availability of funds for new initiatives or continuation of key programs.

3. Labor relations, such as compensation and benefit programs to keep the entity competitive with others in the industry.

Figure 3A.9. Continued.

4. Information systems, such as the adequacy of back-up systems in the event of failure of systems that could significantly affect operations.

Identification of significant risks for each significant activity-level objective. (Consider risks identified with respect to each of the activities identified under "activity-level objectives."

Thoroughness and relevance of the risk analysis process, including estimating the significance of risks, assessing the likelihood of their occurring and determining needed actions. For example, consider whether:

1. Risks are analyzed through formal processes or informal day-to-day management activities.

2. The identified risks are relevant to the corresponding activity objective.

3. Appropriate levels of management are involved in analyzing the risks.

Conclusions/Actions Needed

Managing Change

Economic, industry and regulatory environments change and entities' activities evolve. Mechanisms are needed to identify and react to changing conditions.

Existence of mechanisms to anticipate, identify and react to routine events or activities that affect achievement of entity or activity-level objectives (usually implemented by managers responsible for the activities that would be most affected by the changes). For example, consider whether:

1. Routine changes are addressed as part of the normal risk identification and analysis process, or through separate mechanisms.

2. Risks and opportunities related to the changes are addressed at sufficiently high levels in the organization so their full implications are identified and appropriate action plans formulated.

3. All entity activities significantly affected by the change are brought into the process.

Existence of mechanisms to identify and react to changes that can have a more dramatic and pervasive effect on the entity, and may demand the attention of top management. For example, for each of the following areas of potential change, consider whether:

Figure 3A.9. Continued.

44

Changed operating environment:

1. Market research or other programs identify major shifts in customer demographics, preferences or spending patterns.

2. The entity is aware of significant shifts in the workforce--externally or internally--that could affect available skill levels.

3. Legal counsel periodically updates management on the implications of new legislation.

New personnel:

1. Special action is taken to ensure new personnel understand the entity's culture and perform accordingly.

2. Consideration is given to key control activities performed by personnel being moved.

New or redesigned information systems:

1. Mechanisms exist to assess the effects of new systems.

2. Procedures are in place to reconsider the appropriateness of existing control activities when new computer systems are developed and go "live."

3. Management knows whether systems development and implementation policies are adhered to despite pressures to "short-cut" the process.

4. Attention is given to the effect of new systems on information flows and related controls, and employee training, including focus on employee resistance to change.

Rapid growth:

1. Systems capability is upgraded to handle rapidly increasing volumes of information.

2. Workforce in operations, accounting and data processing is expanded as needed to keep pace with increased volume.

3. A process for revising budgets or forecasts exists.

4. A process exists for considering interdepartmental implications of revised unit objectives and plans.

Figure 3A.9. Continued.

New technology:

1. Information on technological developments is obtained through reporting services, consultants, seminars or perhaps joint ventures with companies in the forefront of research and development relevant to the entity.

2. New technologies, or applications, developed by competitors are monitored.

3. Mechanisms exist for taking advantage, and controlling the use, of new technology applications, incorporating them into production processes or information systems.

New lines, products, activities and acquisitions:

1. The ability exists to reasonably forecast operating and financial results.

2. The adequacy of existing information systems and control activities for the new line, product or activity is assessed.

3. Plans are developed for recruiting and training people with the requisite expertise to deal with new products or activities.

4. Procedures are in place to track early results, and to modify production and marketing as needed.

5. Financial reporting, legal and regulatory requirements are identified and complied with.

6. The effects on other company products, and on profitability, are monitored.

7. Overhead allocations are modified to reflect product contribution accurately.

Corporate restructuring:

1. Staff reassignments or reductions are analyzed for their potential effect on related operations.

2. Transferred or terminated employees' control responsibilities are reassigned.

3. Impact on morale of remaining employees, after major downsizing, considered.

4. Safeguards exist to protect against disgruntled former employees.

Foreign operations:

1. Management keeps abreast of the political, regulatory, business and social culture of areas in which foreign operations exist.

Figure 3A.9. Continued.

2. Personnel are made aware of accepted customs and rules.

3. Alternative procedures exist in case activities of or communication mechanisms with foreign operations are interrupted.

Conclusions/Actions Needed

Component Summary--Conclusions/Actions Needed

Figure 3A.9. Continued.

Internal Control Policy/Procedure

◄ HB ENTERPRISES ►

Chief Executive Office

- RETRIEVAL NO.   502
- PAGE   1 of 2
- ISSUE DATE   January 3, 1994
- DISTRIBUTION   Dept. Heads
- SUPERSEDES

SUBJECT: EVALUATION TOOLS - CONTROL ACTIVITIES

The five internal control components are Control Environment, Risk Assessment, Control Activities, Information and Communication, and Monitoring. This statement covers the evaluation tools for the Control Activities component.

These evaluation tools are intended to provide guidance and assistance in evaluating internal control systems in relation to criteria for effective internal control set forth in the "Framework" volume of Internal Control—Integrated Framework.

These tools are presented for *purely illustrative* purposes, and their presentation here *in no way* suggests that all matters addressed in them need to be considered in evaluating an internal control system, or that all such matters must be present in order to conclude that a system is effective. We may use different evaluation tools, or use other methodologies utilizing different evaluative techniques.

Included under each point of focus (in bold type) are examples of subsidiary issues that might be considered in addressing the point of focus. It is important to recognize that only a *few* examples of such subsidiary issues are provided. Many others usually are relevant. The examples provided are intended only to illustrate the *types* of items to consider.

The evaluator addresses each point of focus, considering the example subsidiary issues as well as others not presented. Although one could record a response for each example subsidiary issue, it is suggested that a response be provided only to the point of focus. The forms to be used will include a "description/comments" column to provide space to record a description of how matters addressed in the point of focus are applied in the entity, and to record relevant comments. The response generally will not be a "yes" or "no" answer, but rather information on how the entity addresses the matter. Following is the Evaluation Form layout:

EVALUATION FORM   AREA OF STUDY_____

POINTS OF FOCUS	DESCRIPTION/COMMENTS
(Description of points to be considered)	(Evaluator's study comments)

At the end of each section is a space to record a conclusion on the effectiveness of the related controls, and any actions that might need to be taken or considered. Space is provided at the end of each tool for similar information on the entire component.

Figure 3A.10.   Statement on evaluation tools—control activities.

CONTROL ACTIVITIES - POINTS OF FOCUS

Control activities encompass a wide range of policies and the related implementation procedures that help ensure that management's directives are effected. They help ensure that those actions identified as necessary to address risks to achieve the entity's objectives are carried out.

Existence of appropriate policies and procedures necessary with respect to each of the entity's activities.

All relevant objectives and associated risks for each significant activity should have been identified in conjunction with evaluating Risk Assessment. Reference may be made to the COSO volume <u>Evaluation Tools</u>, Reference Manual section (pages 57 to 129) which presents, for common business activities, illustrative objectives, risks, and "points of focus for actions/control activities." The listings in that latter column may be useful in identifying what actions management has directed to address the risks, and considering the appropriateness of control activities the entity applies to see that the actions are carried out. It should be recognized that points of focus for general controls (or general computer controls) are presented in the Reference Manual under the activity "Manage Information Technology."

Identified control activities in place are being applied properly. For example, consider whether:

1. Controls described in policy manuals are actually applied and are applied the way that they're supposed to be.

2. Appropriate and timely action is taken on exceptions or information that requires follow-up.

3. Supervisory personnel review the functioning of controls.

Component Summary--Conclusions/Actions Needed

Figure 3A.10. Continued.

◄ HB ENTERPRISES ►

Chief Executive Office

SUBJECT: EVALUATION TOOLS - INFORMATION AND COMMUNICATION

The five internal control components are Control Environment, Risk Assessment, Control Activities, Information and Communication, and Monitoring. This statement covers the evaluation tools for the Information and Communication component.

These evaluation tools are intended to provide guidance and assistance in evaluating internal control systems in relation to criteria for effective internal control set forth in the "Framework" volume of Internal Control—Integrated Framework.

These tools are presented for *purely illustrative* purposes, and their presentation here *in no way* suggests that all matters addressed in them need to be considered in evaluating an internal control system, or that all such matters must be present in order to conclude that a system is effective. We may use different evaluation tools, or use other methodologies utilizing different evaluative techniques.

Included under each point of focus (in bold type) are examples of subsidiary issues that might be considered in addressing the point of focus. It is important to recognize that only a *few* examples of such subsidiary issues are provided. Many others usually are relevant. The examples provided are intended only to illustrate the *types* of items to consider.

The evaluator addresses each point of focus, considering the example subsidiary issues as well as others not presented. Although one could record a response for each example subsidiary issue, it is suggested that a response be provided only to the point of focus. The forms to be used will include a "description/comments" column to provide space to record a description of how matters addressed in the point of focus are applied in the entity, and to record relevant comments. The response generally will not be a "yes" or "no" answer, but rather information on how the entity addresses the matter. Following is the Evaluation Form layout:

EVALUATION FORM   AREA OF STUDY_____

POINTS OF FOCUS	DESCRIPTION/COMMENTS
(Description of points to be considered)	(Evaluator's study comments)

At the end of each section is a space to record a conclusion on the effectiveness of the related controls, and any actions that might need to be taken or considered. Space is provided at the end of each tool for similar information on the entire component.

Figure 3A.11.   Statement on evaluation tools—information and communication.

INFORMATION AND COMMUNICATION - POINTS OF FOCUS

Information

Information is identified, captured, processed and reported by information systems. Relevant information includes industry, economic and regulatory information obtained from external sources, as well as internally generated information.

Obtaining external and internal information, and providing management with necessary reports on the entity's performance relative to established objectives. For example, consider whether:

1. Mechanisms are in place to obtain relevant external information--on market conditions, competitors' programs, legislative or regulatory developments and economic changes.

2. Internally generated information critical to achievement of the entity's objectives, including that relative to critical success factors, is identified and regularly reported.

3. Information that managers need to carry out their responsibilities is reported to them.

Providing information to the right people in sufficient detail and on time to enable them to carry out their responsibilities efficiently and effectively. For example, consider whether:

1. Managers receive analytical information that enables them to identify what action needs to be taken.

2. Information is provided at the right level of detail for different levels of management.

3. Information is summarized appropriately, providing pertinent information while permitting closer inspection of details as needed rather than just a "sea of data."

4. Information is available on a timely basis to allow effective monitoring of events and activities--internal and external--and prompt reaction to economic and business factors and control issues.

Development or revision of information systems based on a strategic plan for information systems--linked to the entity's overall strategy--and responsive to achieving the entity-wide and activity-level objectives. For example, consider whether:

1. A mechanism (e.g., an information technology steering committee) is in place for identifying emerging information needs.

2. Information needs and priorities are determined by executives with sufficiently broad responsibilities.

Figure 3A.11. Continued.

3.   A long-range information technology plan has been developed and linked with strategic initiatives.

Management's support for the development of necessary information systems is demonstrated by the commitment of appropriate resources--human and financial. For example, consider whether:

1.   Sufficient resources (managers, analysts, programmers with the requisite technical abilities) are provided as needed to develop new or enhanced information systems.

Conclusions/Actions Needed

Communication

Communication is inherent in information processing. Communication also takes place in a broader sense, dealing with expectations and responsibilities of individuals and groups. Effective communication must occur down, across and up an organization and with parties external to the organization.

Effectiveness with which employees' duties and control responsibilities are communicated.   For example, consider whether:

1.   Communication vehicles--formal and informal training sessions, meetings and on-the-job supervision--are sufficient in effecting such communication.

2.   Employees know the objectives of their own activity and how their duties contribute to achieving those objectives.

3.   Employees understand how their duties affect, and are affected by, duties of other employees.

Establishment of channels of communication for people to report suspected improprieties. For example, consider whether:

1.   There's a way to communicate upstream through someone other than a direct superior, such as an ombudsman or corporate counsel.

2.   Anonymity is permitted.

3.   Employees actually use the communication channel.

Figure 3A.11.   Continued.

52

4. Persons who report suspected improprieties are provided feedback, and have immunity from reprisals.

Receptivity of management to employee suggestions of ways to enhance productivity, quality or other similar improvements. For example, consider whether:

1. Realistic mechanisms are in place for employees to provide recommendations for improvement.

2. Management acknowledges good employee suggestions by providing cash awards or other meaningful recognition.

Adequacy of communication across the organization (for example, between procurement and production activities) and the completeness and timeliness of information and its sufficiency to enable people to discharge their responsibilities effectively. For example, consider whether:

1. Salespeople inform engineering, production and marketing of customer needs.

2. Accounts receivable personnel advise the credit approval function of slow payers.

3. Information on competitors' new products or warranties reach engineering, marketing and sales personnel.

Openness and effectiveness of channels with customers, suppliers and other external parties for communicating information on changing customer needs. For example, consider whether:

1. Feedback mechanisms with all pertinent parties exist.

2. Suggestions, complaints and other input are captured and communicated to relevant internal parties.

3. Information is reported upstream as necessary and follow-up action taken.

Extent to which outside parties have been made aware of the entity's ethical standards. For example, consider whether:

1. Important communications to outside parties are delivered by management level commensurate with the nature and importance of the message (e.g., senior executive periodically explains in writing the entity's ethical standards to outside parties).

2. Suppliers, customers and others know the entity's standards and expectations regarding actions in dealing with the entity.

Figure 3A.11. Continued.

3. Such standards are reinforced in routine dealings with outside parties.

4. Improprieties by employees of external parties are reported to the appropriate personnel.

Timely and appropriate follow-up action by management resulting from communications received from customers, vendors, regulators or other external parties. For example, consider whether:

1. Personnel are receptive to reported problems regarding products, services or other matters, and such reports are investigated and acted upon.

2. Errors in customer billings are corrected, and the source of the error is investigated and corrected.

3. Appropriate personnel--independent of those involved with the original transactions--process complaints.

4. Appropriate actions are taken and there is follow-up communication with the original sources.

5. Top management is aware of the nature and volume of complaints.

Conclusions/Actions Needed

Component Summary--Conclusions/Actions Needed

Figure 3A.11.   Continued.

Internal Control Policy/Procedure

◄ HB ENTERPRISES ►

Chief Executive Office

• RETRIEVAL NO.   504
•
• PAGE   1 of 5
•
• ISSUE DATE   January 3, 1994
•
• DISTRIBUTION   Dept. Heads
•
• SUPERSEDES

SUBJECT: EVALUATION TOOLS - MONITORING

The five internal control components are Control Environment, Risk Assessment, Control Activities, Information and Communication, and Monitoring. This statement covers the evaluation tools for the Monitoring component.

These evaluation tools are intended to provide guidance and assistance in evaluating internal control systems in relation to criteria for effective internal control set forth in the "Framework" volume of Internal Control—Integrated Framework.

These tools are presented for *purely illustrative* purposes, and their presentation here *in no way* suggests that all matters addressed in them need to be considered in evaluating an internal control system, or that all such matters must be present in order to conclude that a system is effective. We may use different evaluation tools, or use other methodologies utilizing different evaluative techniques.

Included under each point of focus (in bold type) are examples of subsidiary issues that might be considered in addressing the point of focus. It is important to recognize that only a *few* examples of such subsidiary issues are provided. Many others usually are relevant. The examples provided are intended only to illustrate the *types* of items to consider.

The evaluator addresses each point of focus, considering the example subsidiary issues as well as others not presented. Although one could record a response for each example subsidiary issue, it is suggested that a response be provided only to the point of focus. The forms to be used will include a "description/comments" column to provide space to record a description of how matters addressed in the point of focus are applied in the entity, and to record relevant comments. The response generally will not be a "yes" or "no" answer, but rather information on how the entity addresses the matter. Following is the Evaluation Form layout:

EVALUATION FORM   AREA OF STUDY_____

POINTS OF FOCUS	DESCRIPTION/COMMENTS
(Description of points to be considered)	(Evaluator's study comments)

At the end of each section is a space to record a conclusion on the effectiveness of the related controls, and any actions that might need to be taken or considered. Space is provided at the end of each tool for similar information on the entire component.

Figure 3A.12.   Statement on evaluation tools—monitoring.

MONITORING - POINTS OF FOCUS

Ongoing Monitoring

Ongoing monitoring occurs in the ordinary course of operations, and includes regular management and supervisory activities, and other actions personnel take in performing their duties that assess the quality of internal control system performance.

Extent to which personnel, in carrying out their regular activities, obtain evidence as to whether the system of internal control continues to function. For example, consider whether:

1. Operating management compares production, inventory, sales or other information obtained in the course of their daily activities to systems-generated information.

2. Integration or reconciliation of operating information used to manage operations with data generated by the financial reporting system.

3. Operating personnel are required to "sign off" on the accuracy of their units' financial statements, and are held responsible if errors are discovered.

Extent to which communications from external parties corroborate internally generated information, or indicate problems. For example, consider whether:

1. Customers implicitly corroborate billing data by paying their invoices, or customer complaints about billings--indicating system deficiencies in the processing of sales transactions--are investigated for their underlying causes.

2. Communications from vendors and monthly statements of accounts payable are used as a control monitoring technique.

3. Suppliers' complaints of unfair practices by purchasing agents are fully investigated.

4. Regulators communicate information to the entity regarding compliance or other matters that reflect on the functioning of the internal control system.

5. Controls that should have prevented or detected the problems are reassessed.

Periodic comparison of amounts recorded by the accounting system with physical assets. For example, consider whether:

1. Inventory levels are checked when goods are taken from inventory storage for shipment, and differences between recorded and actual amounts are corrected.

2. Securities held in trust are counted periodically and compared with existing records.

Figure 3A.12. Continued.

Responsiveness to internal and external auditor recommendations on means to strengthen internal controls. For example, consider whether:

1. Executives with proper authority decide which of the auditors' recommendations will be implemented.

2. Desired actions are followed up to verify implementation.

Extent to which training seminars, planning sessions and other meetings provide feedback to management on whether controls operate effectively. For example, consider whether:

1. Relevant issues and questions raised at training seminars are captured.

2. Employee suggestions are communicated upstream and acted on as appropriate.

Whether personnel are asked periodically to state whether they understand and comply with the entity's code of conduct and regularly perform critical control activities. For example, consider whether:

1. Personnel are required periodically to acknowledge compliance with the code of conduct.

2. Signatures are required to evidence performance of critical control functions, such as reconciling specified amounts.

Effectiveness of internal audit activities. For example, consider whether:

1. There are appropriate levels of competent and experienced staff.

2. Their position within the organization is appropriate.

3. They have access to the board of directors or audit committee.

4. Their scope, responsibilities and audit plans are appropriate to the organization's needs.

Conclusions/Actions Needed

Separate Evaluations

It is useful to take a fresh look at the internal control system from time to time, focusing directly on system effectiveness. The scope and frequency of separate evaluations will depend primarily on an assessment of risks, and ongoing monitoring procedures.

Figure 3A.12. Continued.

Scope and frequency of separate evaluations of the internal control system. For example, consider whether:

1. Appropriate portions of the internal control system are evaluated.

2. The evaluations are conducted by personnel with the requisite skills.

3. The scope, depth of coverage and frequency are adequate.

Appropriateness of the evaluation process. For example, consider whether:

1. The evaluator gains a sufficient understanding of the entity's activities.

2. An understanding is obtained of how the system is supposed to work and how it actually does work.

3. An analysis is made, using the evaluation results as measured against established criteria.

Whether the methodology for evaluating a system is logical and appropriate. For example, consider whether:

1. Such methodology includes checklists, questionnaires or other tools.

2. The evaluation team is brought together to plan the evaluation process and ensure a coordinated effort.

3. The evaluation process is managed by an executive with requisite authority.

Appropriateness of the level of documentation. For example, consider whether:

1. Policy manuals, organization charts, operating instructions and the like are available.

2. Consideration is given to documenting the evaluation process.

Conclusions/Actions Needed

Reporting Deficiencies

Internal control deficiencies should be reported upstream with certain matters reported to top management and the board.

Figure 3A.12. Continued.

Existence of mechanism for capturing and reporting identified internal control deficiencies. For example, consider whether means exist for obtaining reports on deficiencies:

1. From both internal sources and external sources (e.g., customers, suppliers, auditors, regulators).

2. Resulting from ongoing monitoring or separate evaluations.

Appropriateness of reporting protocols. For example, consider whether:

1. Deficiencies are reported to the person directly responsible for the activity and to a person at least one level higher.

2. Specified types of deficiencies are reported to more senior management and to the board.

Appropriateness of follow-up actions. For example, consider whether:

1. The transaction or event identified is corrected.

2. The underlying causes of the problem are investigated.

3. There is follow-up to ensure the necessary corrective action is taken.

Conclusions/Actions Needed

Component Summary--Conclusions/Actions Needed

Figure 3A.12. Continued.

Internal Control Policy/Procedure	• RETRIEVAL NO. 505
	•
	• PAGE Page 1 of 1
◄ HB ENTERPRISES ►	•
	• ISSUE DATE January 4, 1994
	•
Chief Executive Office	• DISTRIBUTION Dept. Heads
	•
	• SUPERSEDES

SUBJECT: RISK ASSESSMENT AND CONTROL ACTIVITIES WORKSHEET

As noted in the evaluation tools for Risk Assessment and Control Activities, management establishes objectives for *each* significant activity; analyzes risks to their achievement; establishes plans, programs and other actions to address the risks; and puts in place control activities to ensure that the actions are carried out. The tools for Risk Assessment and Control Activities do not provide a vehicle to evaluate this process at the activity level. A separate worksheet is provided to assist in this regard.

Management may or may not have already documented this process. If not, the worksheet provides a vehicle to assist management in performing and documenting the process. An evaluator then can review the completed worksheet. If management has no documentation, the evaluator might consider preparing the worksheet (with the assistance of management) in order to evaluate the process and associated linkages.

The Reference Manual of the "Evaluation Tools" volume of Internal Control - Integrated Framework (page 49) is designed to assist in identifying activity-level objectives, analyzing the risks, and determining what actions might be taken and what control activities put in place.

The attached reduced copy the Worksheet illustrates how the form is used. The column O,F,C has been deleted from the original form as it seems to serve little purpose and complicates the process of completing the form following a review of a specific internal control function. It is understood that a "Program of Examination" of the specific unit or function to be reviewed is prepared before starting the review.

Attachment: Partially completed Risk Assessment and Control Activities Worksheet.

Figure 3A.13. Statement on risk assessment and control activities worksheet.

Activity __INBOUND MATERIALS__

Objectives	Risk Analysis		Actions/ Control Activities/	Other Objectives Affected	Evaluation and Conclusion
	Risk Factors	Likelihood	Comments		
Manage Logistics					
1. Materials are to be tested, and either accepted or moved to storage, or rejected and returned for credit on a timely basis.	Receipt of large quantities of materials may delay the receiving and testing activities.	Medium-High	1. Production provides a weekly report of those items most critically needed to continue efficient and uninterrupted production. The Director of Procurement reviews materials to be tested and prioritizes such materials based on the weekly report. 2. Certain engineering personnel have been trained and are available for short-term use in testing certain types of materials.		Policies and procedures are insufficient for timely processing. Policies and procedures must be developed to detail how materials should flow through receiving and testing, in the event of large amounts of material being received, and how the achievement of the objective is to be monitored. Additionally, using engineering personnel to test materials may create conflicts between testing and engineering, especially if such use negatively affects achievement of engineering objectives.
2. Accurately process all information related to goods received, and make such information available to appropriate activities on a timely basis.	Information is not entered accurately or on a timely basis.	Medium	3. Receiving reports are prenumbered, and missing documents are investigated twice weekly.		Controls are sufficient to achieve the objective.

Note: This example of an evaluation tool is filled in for one activity of ABC Company. When evaluating the risk assessment and control activities company-wide, this tool would be completed for all significant activities.

Figure 3A.13. Continued.

61

Internal Control Policy/Procedure

◄ HB ENTERPRISES ►

Chief Executive Office

- RETRIEVAL NO.   506
- PAGE   1 of 2
- ISSUE DATE   January 4, 1994
- DISTRIBUTION   Dept. Heads
- SUPERSEDES

SUBJECT: OVERALL INTERNAL CONTROL SYSTEM EVALUATION

This final evaluation tool is provided to summarize the findings and conclusions for each of the components. It also facilitates the review of the preliminary results by more senior executives who may add further information. Space for an overall conclusion on the internal control system is provided.

The form is completed as follows:

Internal Control Components. Completed by the evaluation team based on the initial objectives and plans for the review.

Preliminary Conclusions/Actions Needed. Also completed by the evaluation team based on the results of the Risk Assessment and Control Activities Worksheets.

Additional Considerations. This space provided for comments by the CEO, a board member, or other senior officers on the completed evaluation as described by the evaluation team on this form.

Figure 3A.14. Statement on overall internal control system evaluation.

Overall Internal Control System Evaluation

Internal Control Components	Preliminary Conclusions/ Actions Needed (see individual evaluation tools)

Control Environment.

Does management adequately convey the message that integrity cannot be compromised? Does a positive control environment exist? Is the competence of the entity's people commensurate with their responsibilities? Are management's operating style, the way it assigns authority and responsibility and organizes and develops is people appropriate? Does the board provide the right level of attention?

Management has demonstrated its commitment to integrity, ethical behavior and competence of the Company's people, and has communicated that commitment to all employees. The Company's control environment is conducive to effective internal control, and provides a positive influence that enhances the likelihood of achieving ABC's objectives.

Additional Considerations

The board and I (CEO) are considering the benefits of a formal code of conduct. I am monitoring the effectiveness of the recent organizational structure modifications and will introduce changes as appropriate. Reviews of personnel requirements are underway.

Risk Assessment
  (Complete as above)

Control Activities
  (Complete as above)

Information and Communication
  (Complete as above)

Monitoring
  (Complete as above)

Overall Conclusion

ABC's system of internal control, as of December 31, 19xx, is effective and provides reasonable assurance that the company's financial reporting process is reliable, that the company has effective procedures for ensuring compliance with applicable laws and regulations, and that management is aware of the extent to which the company is moving toward achieving the operations objectives.

Figure 3A.14. Continued.

CHAPTER 6
DATA PROCESSING
MANUAL:
PUT YOUR RIGHT
DATA OUT

Page 152, add before Summary:

DOCUMENTING PERSONAL COMPUTER OPERATIONS (NEW)

More and more data processing is being done on the microcomputer, better known as the personal computer (PC), and there is less reliance on the large mainframe computer. The PC can be either a stand-alone processor or one tied into a network system. In the stand-alone mode, both programs and data files are stored in the PC and results are printed at that station. In a network mode, the programs may be stored in the mainframe and called into the PC when needed. Data may also be stored in the mainframe or on the hard disk in the PC. Printing may be done locally or at a remote printer.

Master Program Backup

If the programs are stored in the mainframe computer, the programmer-analyst is responsible for backing up the programs in case of loss. If they are stored in the PC, the local operator-user should maintain a copy of the current programs for use in case of loss (the master program should be stored at another location in case of a catastrophic loss by fire or other similar event). If lost, it is a simple matter to install the master program from the copy thereof (which names the directory) and then add the current data backup files to the directory.

Data Backup

For current data such as calculated worksheets, accounting transactions, or word processing output (letters, reports, and so forth), the local user of the PC is responsible for backing up the files. The rule for backing up any data is that if the data would be difficult to reconstruct, usually because the original documents were not printed as updated or have been filed and it is time-consuming to locate and re-enter, then backing up the files should be frequent *and* mandatory on a fixed schedule.

Every program that updates an existing file or saves a newly produced file should end with a file-closing routine that reminds the user to save the file or files. Following is a sample closing routine:

1. At the exiting routine, the screen should resemble Figure 6.11A.

Backup Routine

Do you want to backup data files? Y/N? --

If yes, place formatted backup disk in backup disk drive.

Figure 6.11A.

2. Answer "Y" and the screen in Figure 6.11B appears.
3. Enter backup disk drive to be used. If backup location is correct, press "Y" and the screen in Figure 6.11C appears.
4. If the old backup file is a grandfather version and no longer needed, press "Y" and the files are backed up and listed in rotation, followed by the screen shown in Figure 6.11D.
5. Press any key and the screen returns to the basic C:> prompt.

Drive to place backup data files ? A:\ or B:\? --

Above backup path correct? Y/N? --

Formatted backup disk in backup disk drive.

Figure 6.11B.

Location to place backup data files ? A:\

Files are already in backup location.

Overwrite them ? Y

Figure 6.11C.

Data files to backup = 4

Files copied = 4

Backup complete - Any key ->

Figure 6.11D.

If only one or two files are to be saved, use the DOS command "Copy" followed by the drive and pathname of the file to be copied and the drive to be copied to. For example, to copy a file named "HARRYMS.TXT," filed under directory "MYDATA" and subdirectory "WILEY," to a diskette in drive A, the command would be:

COPY C:\MYDATA\WILEY\HARRYMS.TXT A:

The reminder at every file-closing routine causes me to back up the working files much more frequently than if no reminder existed. Because of the simplicity, I use two backup floppy disks to back up my files, each with the backup date on the sleeve label. The oldest dated disk is used whenever a new backup procedure is performed. Thus, two sets of backup files are always available.

Backup of vital records and files is absolutely necessary. The organization should issue a P/PS to notify all PC users, whether stand-alone or networked, to back up their files frequently, preferably after each update of formulas, data, or word processing operations.

CHAPTER 10
STYLE:
THE EASY WRITER

Page 279, add at end of section:

COMMON GRAMMAR AND USAGE PROBLEMS

Abbreviations are common in technical manuals. Used judiciously, they increase readability by making the writing more concise. Overuse, however, may lead to cryptic writing that the reader must "decode." Choose the *standard* abbreviation for a term and use it *consistently*.

If you must use an abbreviation that may be unfamiliar to your reader, write it out at first mention.

Spell out "that is," "for example," "and so on," and "versus." Their abbreviations (i.e., e.g., etc., vs.) are acceptable, though, when they occur with material within parentheses.

Spell out "United States," except before the name of a government department or bureau, vessel, road, and patent number, in quoted material, and in crowded tables.

United States government

In the United States

U.S. Bureau of Standards

U.S.S. *Maine*

U.S. Patent 2,867,567

U.S. 45

Spell out names of the states, territories, and possessions of the United States, except in quoted material, crowded tables, footnotes and references after the name of a city, and addresses. Much of the mail handled by the U.S. Postal Service is read by optical character recognition software and then converted to an 11-digit delivery point barcode. Mail addresses should be in all capital letters with no punctuation. See Figure 10.5 for approved standard postal abbreviations.

Omit the period in acronyms (abbreviations formed with the initial letters of words):

CPA

USA

ESP

MOS

AFL-CIO

AT&T

SEC

UNESCO

The period is becoming optional in many abbreviations. Compare the two columns:

Ph.D	PhD
M.D.	MD
2:45 P.M.	2:45 PM
6:30 A.M.	6:30 AM
A.D. 1980	AD 1980
2000 B.C.	2000 BC

Quotation Marks.   Double quotation marks should be used for excerpts. Periods and commas fall *inside* quotation marks. Colons and semicolons fall *outside*.

Ellipses.   Three dots (. . .) indicate that material is deleted at the beginning of or within a sentence. Four dots (. . . .) indicate that material is deleted at the end of a sentence (the extra dot accounts for the period).

Hyphens.   Hyphens should be used cautiously. Many noun combinations that formerly were hyphenated are now written as solid words: butterfat, willpower, patternmaker. Some nouns are still hyphenated (well-being), and some that once were hyphenated are now two words (water supply). The hyphens in trademarks must be retained: Coca-Cola. The writing of fast-developing scientific and technical terminology

Alabama	AL	Montana	MT	Avenue	AVE
Alaska	AK	Nebraska	NE	Boulevard	BLVD
Arizona	AZ	Nevada	NV	Court	CT
Arkansas	AR	New Hampshire	NH	Center	CTR
California	CA	New Jersey	NJ	Circle	CIR
Colorado	CO	New Mexico	NM	Drive	DR
Connecticut	CT	New York	NY	Expressway	EXPY
Delaware	DE	North Carolina	NC	Heights	HTS
Dist. of Col.	DC	North Dakota	ND	Highway	HWY
Florida	FL	Ohio	OH	Island	IS
Georgia	GA	Oklahoma	OK	Junction	JCT
Guam	GU	Oregon	OR	Lake	LK
Hawaii	HI	Pennsylvania	PA	Lane	LN
Idaho	ID	Puerto Rico	PR	Mountain	MTN
Illinois	IL	Rhode Island	RI	Parkway	PKY
Indiana	IN	South Carolina	SC	Place	PL
Iowa	IA	South Dakota	SD	Road	RD
Kansas	KS	Tennessee	TN	Station	STA
Kentucky	KY	Texas	TX	Street	ST
Louisiana	LA	Utah	UT	Turnpike	TPKE
Maine	ME	Vermont	VT	Valley	VLY
Maryland	MD	Virginia	VA	Apartment	APT
Massachusetts	MA	Virgin Islands	VI	Room	RM
Michigan	MI	Washington	WA	Suite	STE
Minnesota	MN	West Virginia	WV	Plaza	PLZ
Mississippi	MS	Wisconsin	WI	North	N
Missouri	MO	Wyoming	WY	East	E
				South	S
				West	W

Figure 10.5. Standard U.S. Postal Service abbreviations.

is especially subject to change. Keep a copy of the current edition of *Webster's New Collegiate Dictionary* on your desk for easy reference when necessary.

Capitalization. Capital letters indicate the beginnings of sentences, proper nouns and adjectives, and precise titles.

In writing your manuals, distinguish between such general titles as "federal government" or "state government" and such precise titles as "the U.S. Congress," "Michigan State Senate." Do not capitalize for irony or some other special effect.

The names of legislative acts are capitalized, however: Civil Rights Act of 1964.

Capitalize trademarks: Xerox, Coca-Cola. Only the initial letter of each word is capitalized.

In capital-letter **titles** and **headings** capitalize as follows:

- Capitalize the second word in a hyphenated expression regardless of its form and meaning: Twentieth-Century Technology; Fuel-Burning Equipment; Drive-In Theater.
- Capitalize acronyms (abbreviations formed by initial letters) even if they are lowercased in the text: Characteristics of CPA Candidates.

Prefixes and Suffixes.   Most prefixes and suffixes are closed up.

foresight	postaudit
lifelike	pretax
microfilm	pretest
nonprofit	semifinal
outpatient	socioeconomic
photoreproduction	subgroup

SUPPLEMENT INDEX